Richard Deatherage was born in Santa Maria, California. Being versatile in his career, he is a finish carpenter, architectural draftsman, builder and avid fly fisherman... building large commercial projects throughout the west coast of the United States of America. Disguised as a construction superintendent, Richard works for large contractors, and goes fly fishing every chance he can throughout the Pacific Northwest, Washington, Oregon, California, and Nevada. He lives in Northern California.

This book is dedicated to my parents, Charles and Teresa Deatherage. As a young child, I witnessed the trials and tribulations of the late '60s and early '70s… remembering the resilience and strength of parents who raised me, and three siblings on a single income military budget during the Vietnam war, and beyond. During inflation that put the nation on its heals during the mid-70s. I remembered our story, it inspired me and gave me the strength to carry on during my own struggles during the 2008 recession…

Richard Deatherage

AN AMERICAN STAIRWAY

AUSTIN MACAULEY PUBLISHERS™

LONDON • CAMBRIDGE • NEW YORK • SHARJAH

Ordering Information
Quantity sales: Special discounts are available on quantity purchases by corporations, associations, and others. For details, contact the publisher at the address below.

Publisher's Cataloging-in-Publication data
Deatherage, Richard
An American Stairway

ISBN 9798891552241 (Paperback)
ISBN 9798891552258 (ePub e-book)

Library of Congress Control Number: 2023921040

www.austinmacauley.com/us

First Published 2024
Austin Macauley Publishers LLC
40 Wall Street, 33rd Floor, Suite 3302
New York, NY 10005
USA

mail-usa@austinmacauley.com
+1 (646) 5125767

To my parents, who told me of our family's unknown stories
to complete this book.

American stairways are full of them, pictures from our past with the stories they can tell in an instant. Some family members have passed away through time.

Others are still with us, living life, growing older… maybe I should call them, but no… it has been too long. So our snapshots in time go on our American stairway walls to share with others and to dust off the stories of our time.

Richard Deatherage, 2022

Chapter 1
Greatest Fortune

In November of 2008, I was told by my employers that I would be laid off from work by the end of that year, that the construction lending had fallen through for our clients projected for the 2009 construction season.

I was not alone; many companies had been laying off their workers that year and it was not a big surprise to me at the time. It was all over the news that we were in a bad recession and I knew that it was going to get worse after the holiday season.

I had been through a few recessions in the late 1970s and through the early '80s and '90s. I had always worked through them, changing as I needed to from my many past versatile experiences as a carpenter, draftsman, builder and construction superintendent for other builders.

I had always kept adaptable and open to change. But this time, the economic indicators were different. For the first time in my 30-year working career at 46 years of age, I was laid off from work and unemployed with no work to be had, like many millions of others.

I did prepare ahead of time, seeing the inevitable approaching, having been through recessions in the past. My credit was still great and I still had a corporate business that was still active from my previous business adventures, just in case I ever needed it to start a new venture.

At the time, I had two options: I could find another job, which was impossible at that time because no one was hiring. Or I could go into debt, to jumpstart my business to find a client with the cash to design and build their new home. The odds were not good at the time to find the needle in a haystack.

This was the last thing I wanted to do—go into business again and go into debt. I enjoyed working for other large construction firms and I was enjoying not having to worry about draws, meeting payroll, etc.

I was overseeing the construction jobs in the field as a construction superintendent to beat the deadline under time and under budget. I was enjoying the challenge of what I was doing.

I had gone on unemployment after my lay-off and started to receive my unemployment cheques regularly. My wife Sarah was still working as a waitress at the time and she had been a waitress for over 30 years, enjoying what she was doing for a living.

We could pay our mortgage but were unable to budget for my truck payments. So, I had to dip into my 401K to pay off my truck and some credit card debts to pay the mortgage.

After we settled into a new budget to save our home, we could pay all our household bills with $50 to spare each month. We could make it on unemployment and with my wife's income until I could find a new client.

It was a very tight budget and I continued looking for work through the state's unemployment network.

At the same time, my father's health was failing, as he had been diagnosed with the lung disease called pulmonary fibrosis six years prior. It was starting to take a toll on him during the winter months.

I soon found out that being laid off from work was a blessing for me, as well as it being so for our family. I was able to spend more time with my ailing father as we started to plan for the inevitable during a very difficult time in our family's history.

Starting with the remodelling of my parents' bathrooms to be handicap accessible, I was available to help set up a new routine with Mom and Dad, as we planned together for the final outcome that comes with such preparations.

I also had a new drive in my life, a re-evaluation of sorts as I worked on my parents' bathroom remodels. I cherish those moments I had with my father, who supervised the bathroom projects in a role reversal.

My parents' stairway was full of family photos and each time I went up the stairs to remodel the bathrooms, I would stop and look at the photos. I was reminded of the great times that I had had growing up and of all that Mom and Dad had done for my brothers and me.

For in my youth, we had moved every four years all over the United States of America, from air force base to air force base. Up until the time I was 12 years old, I had started to relive all of the amazing adventures my family had been through in the 1960s and 70s.

The family adventures we had and the encouragement we had all been given by my parents over the years as an air force brat was a story lost in time.

I started to reflect on my childhood with my parents growing up and started going over picture albums of all the great memories we had as a family.

All of us boys had started our own families years before, working and living our own lives to come back full circle to the beginning of the end of our father's life.

Looking back, I believe that the freedoms that I had in my life experiences growing up may have held the answers to being happy in life.

Only then can you realise that in life as well as in death, that freedom is one of the greatest fortunes your parents can ever give to you and the grounded life of a good family upbringing is the icing on the cake.

Chapter 2
Burnt Toast

Some of my first memories were of the bite of the bitter cold winters at Ellsworth Air Force Base in Rapid City, South Dakota. I was going on five years old in the winter of 1967, remembering the drifts of snow covering the roads and houses on the air base.

I distinctly remember that my brother Charlie and I were not able to go out the back door to play because the windows and the door on that side of the house were dark with the large snow drifts covering over the roof of our home.

Other first experiences of my youth were seeing my first airplanes flying overhead. I can still hear the jet engines winding up for take-off with the anticipation of soon seeing the B-52s taking off one after another, flying overhead while I was playing outside.

It was an amazing experience at that age seeing so many B-52 bombers flying overhead, going out on missions. It was impressive to see something flying that was so large. It's an image that is still burnt into my mind, even after all these years.

Other vivid memories were of getting in trouble for taking a large black marker pen and scribbling on all the kitchen cabinets and down the hallway walls. It must have left a major impression in my mind to remember that as well. It must have been one of the first times I was scolded severely. My first drawing had gone badly.

In 1968, my father was transferred from the air base in South Dakota and the family moved on to Columbus Air Force Base in Columbus, Mississippi.

Unknown to me at the time, my mom told me later in life that before they had moved to Mississippi, Mom and Dad had to sign papers to say that neither parent would marry outside of their own race for their own safety. This paper was a sign of things to come for our family.

Some of my favourite memories living in Mississippi were of my younger brothers John and Jimmy being born. I remember holding the 8MM camera with my uncle Cam and taking the pictures of each of them coming out of the hospital with my parents, to take them home after their births.

My parents were a very adventurous couple who loved the great outdoors, where camping throughout Mississippi at the time was a way of life for us, where a camping trip was done at the drop of a hat most weekends.

My father, who was born and raised in Barbourville, Kentucky, would take us out on camping and fishing trips throughout Mississippi, telling us stories around the campfire of his childhood.

On one of our camping trips in 1969, there was an unknown brush with death as my dad put it in this story to me, and I remember it as the 'burnt toast' camping trip.

My dad took my brother Charlie and myself out on a camping trip not knowing that Hurricane Camille was on its way to take a swipe through Mississippi.

As the story goes, we went camping to a place called Davis Lake, where all was well until nightfall came and the hurricane hit the tent that we were sleeping in with a vengeance. Dad explained that he had spent all night holding up the tent and tying off the tent with ropes from tree to tree to keep us all from blowing away inside it.

He must have done a great job because Charlie and I slept all night long, not knowing of the hurricane at all.

What I remembered the most from the next morning, after a good night's sleep, was that Dad had burnt the toast at breakfast over the campfire… The poor guy had been up all night trying to save our lives and he had to hear complaints from his well-rested kids about burnt toast!

I distinctly remember him explaining that the burnt toast is not burnt toast if you can scrape off the blackened char and there is brown under the remains of the toast.

I remember scraping off the blackened char with a knife and eating the worst toast of my young life because Dad would not make us any more toast. If we wanted more toast, we had to eat what he had already burnt.

It went on as a family joke not to let Dad toast any bread on any family camping trips for the rest of his life.

We left the camping site to go home from the camping trip from hell, as my dad put it, only to get home to the base housing to find out that the large willow tree that was in our side yard had been blown over in the storm.

Only then did it hit me that the large tree I had played under just days before was now on its side and was gone forever due to the magnitude of the storm from the night before.

Chapter 3
The Hate of Racism

If you think about all the different races of mankind on Earth as we know of them today, the opportunities for all of them to come together began through the efforts of our American military during World War II and through our American Peace Corps through the1960s.

It was the beginning of the end and the gradual breakdown of racism in America from the time of the Civil War. All our military services and the respect they made you have for each other through your rank, no matter what colour you were, had begun.

Whether you were white, black, yellow, red or brown… when you were in the military services, you had better respect the officers in charge no matter what colour they were. Or there was going to be a mark on your service record forever.

Of course, back then we were still in the infancy of race relationships. There was still racism during the Vietnam era and through the 1970s whether we like to admit it or not. Fifty years later, racism still continues to raise its ugly head.

As an older white man today, I had thought that we had turned the page of racism from what I had witnessed as a young child long ago. Never to hear or think about racism again until recently on the news.

For the most part in my earlier life, I grew up as a young white child sheltered, not knowing about people in a way of colour or race from air base to air base, right up until the time I was six years old.

The first black people that I had ever known worked at the local grocery store nearby, with their thick southern drawl being the first language to me that I had to learn how to decipher.

As an air force brat, my English was north-western mostly, using my own father's Kentucky twang as a training tool to help decipher by. I could recognise the drawl at times and if you listened real close… you could catch on over time.

Looking back, the things that I remember the most were good times in Mississippi, camping and fishing. Riding my Schwinn bicycle with a banana seat up and down the streets in base housing.

As kids, we played with clackers, flew June bugs with fishing lines, caught snapping turtles, burnt up large red ants with a magnifying glass and played the newest 45 records with the neighbourhood children.

The vinyl records I remember being played on the turntable at the time were Elvis Presley, the Beatles, the Rolling Stones and the Carpenters. I also remember hearing the blues being played on the radio near our old grocery store.

Mississippi was a beautiful place to live, with the weeping willows having moss falling from the branches of the trees. There were large open spaces, with fields of corn and cotton all around, with locusts and birds singing their songs in the background.

What I remember from being a child in the Mississippi of my youth were great memories for the most part. But seeing racism for the first time burnt an impression in my mind that has lasted to this day and was a lesson on how I would treat and respect others for the rest of my lifetime.

No matter where you grew up in Mississippi, you saw disrespect for black people first hand. It was the littlest things I noticed initially that seemed off to me, not being a native to the area.

The term 'yes, sir, boss man' and the cower of the black man to the white man was prevalent all around… I had started to take notice.

One day, I remember shopping with my mother, walking on the sidewalk, and there was a white man behind us yelling out loudly as a black man approached…

"Hey, boy, you better get off of the sidewalk when you see white folk walking your way!"

At first, I thought he was talking to me until I saw the black man stepping aside in front of us, cowering and saying, "Yes sir, boss man…" as the white man behind us walked by and tipped his hat to my mom and said politely to her, "Have a nice day, mama," while glaring at the black man.

As a small child seeing this, I thought I had never heard that tone of language from one person to another before. The disrespect from one race of man to another I had never seen or heard before as a six-year-old air force brat. I remember thinking, *That was odd.*

Following that, one hot summer day I witnessed the hate of racism for the first time in my young life… It is burnt in my mind forever…

My father and I were at the local gas station, where the service attendant had just completed filling up our family car.

It was hot that day and my father had paid the attendant for the gas and told me that he was going to get a soda for both of us from the soda machine inside the gas station.

He had just gone inside the gas station as the attendant was starting to fill up the car beside us. Another car pulled up quickly, coming to a tire-skidding halt with four young white men in their 20s jumping out of their car at the same time. Two of them were heading to the filling attendant, who was still filling up the other car.

I could see the expression of the filling attendant's face as he was pumping gas into the car. The fear in his face, once he realised what only he must have known was going to happen to him next.

The filling attendant stopped gassing up the car, putting his hands up as he was backing away from the car... "Hey, n_____! You're going to fill my car up first!" shouted one of the white men who had gone up to him, as the other two passengers were getting out of the car laughing, while turning their attention to the man inside the car that was getting his car filled up with gas.

One guy opened up the passenger door of the car and sat in the seat, leaning over and saying something to the driver. The other guy went around, opened the door and pulled out the man sitting in the car. It turned out that he was a black man. After pulling the man out of the car, he pushed him away from his car, daring him to make a move. The smaller frightened man backed down.

The other guy slid over from the passenger's seat to the driver's seat and started up the car and then drove it through the barbed wire fence into the field by the gas station, tearing up dirt, fence and post, spinning 360 degrees with the car in the field, while the other hooligans were doing the rebel yell, screaming to their friend, encouraging him on.

The gas service attendant who had the gas pump handle in his hand said to the owner of the car, "You better leave before they think of something else to do." The man backed off with his hands up in the air, while one of the kids pulled their car into his place. The gas station attendant proceeded to put gas into that car.

The kid who had driven the car into the field got out of the car and walked back to the gas station, pushing the black owner of the car, who pushed back.

That set off a fight that the black man lost when the white kid got a direct hit on the black man's face. He fell to the ground holding his face, while the white kid started kicking him, telling him each time he kicked him: "(*Kick*) Pay (*kick*), for (*kick*), my (*kick*), gas (*kick*), n_______!"

I was in shock seeing this happen. My dad, who came out of the garage area with our sodas in hand, walked up to the filling attendant, who was still filling up their car, and said something to him that I could not hear at the time.

I could not make it out but, years later, my dad told me while going over the story that he had told the gas station attendant that he was a marine and asked the attendant to back my dad up.

Dad gave me the sodas and told me to stay in the car. He walked over to help the man who had been kicked and hurt back up onto his feet… then asked if he was all right. The man said, "Yes, sir, boss man."

My dad then said, "You don't have to call me boss man."

One kid said to my dad, "Hey! Leave that n______ alone!"

Like a lion, my dad roared back while holding the man up and said, "If you want a piece of me... I'm a marine; bring it on, you motherfuckers!"

They all looked surprised! Hell, I was surprised! I had never seen my dad like that before!

Wow!

Instantly backing down, they were all surprised, looking at my dad, who they instantly knew meant business.

The filling attendant stopped the gas flow into their car with the sudden 'thump' of the gas pump stopping as the only sound heard in silence.

The cowards stared at my dad as one of them said, "It's not worth it, guys. We got what we wanted." They backed down, got into their car and drove off.

The lessons I learnt that day were not hard to comprehend. I was going on seven years old the day my father stood up against the racists thugs at that gas station.

The way I felt that day had all the emotions of surprise, fear, shock, sorrow and the tensions of the unknown... I looked at my father in a whole new light, with the respect for a father who stood up for what was right.

If you're full of hate, rage and bulling your way through life, you're going down the wrong path. Someday, someone will stand up to you... It may even be a bystander you don't know... or it may be an old marine with his war face on... Personally, I would not want to be on the receiving end.

I was proud of my father and told him so while going over this event in our lives.

Chapter 4
The Great Unknown

From the time the last of the baby boomer generation started preschool and moved into our public-school systems, our generation stood up, placed our right hands over our hearts and pledged our allegiance to the flag of the United States of America before the start of each school day.

I remember one day when I was in the first grade, our teacher asked us to stand up to say the Pledge of Allegiance. She said it with a broken voice that we had not heard from her before, like she was going to cry.

Suddenly, our teacher started to cry uncontrollably; we were just taken aback why our teacher had started to cry uncontrollably. Some of the children went up to hug her; we were all mesmerised, as to why our teacher was crying.

It was one of those moments that you never forget. Once she regained her composure, she explained that she had had a close friend who had been killed in action recently in the war in Vietnam and that it was his birthday that day.

Then it hit us why she was crying. Once she had calmed down, she stated, "Let's continue on with the Pledge of Allegiance." She explained why we say the pledge. We say the pledge for the respect to all the families who have lived, fought and made sacrifices to make our country a better place to live.

I never forgot what she said because at that time, there were other child in class who had lost a father in the war, as they too were visibly upset, hearing of the news that morning.

We were aware of the possibilities of death from war, as I thought of my father who was soon going to the war in Vietnam.

When Dad got his orders to be sent to Vietnam, unknown to my parents, when you were sent to Vietnam, your privilege of the air base housing was all but over and there was another family moving in to your air base home pretty dammed quick (PDQ).

My parents had to scramble to move us off the base housing that summer before Dad was sent overseas. I remember going with my parents to the mobile home factory sales offices and walking through trailer home after trailer home until they found the one that they liked.

Unknown to me at the time, my dad had to borrow some money from my grandparents, who lived in Knoxville, Tennessee, to help make the deposit on the purchase.

Soon, we were ready to move from the air base housing to a local trailer park outside the protection of Columbus Air Force Base boundaries.

To a child who had never lived outside of the safety of base housing, it was the little things that I remembered the most.

We did not have to go through a guarded gate to get home anymore. There was no covered porch out the front door. There was a wooden deck landing, with stairs out the front door and out the back door. I could crawl under the house all the way through to the other side.

Soon, there were other trailers moving in all around the park with new children to play with, while other military families were moving in quickly.

My dad had completed getting us settled into our new home and it did not seem too long after we were settled in that Dad was packing up and getting ready to be sent to Vietnam.

I remember taking my dad to the airport to leave for Vietnam. It was nothing like the major airports of today. You simply drove through the parking lot of the airport, where the planes were taxied. Mom drove up to the three-foot high fence that surrounded the airfield and you could park the car wherever you wanted to.

Dad got out of the car, gave us all a big hug and told me that I was the oldest and in charge until he got back. Then he walked through the open space in the fence, where he walked up to the base of the steps, going up into the plane.

There was a man who was holding a clipboard at the base of the steps. Dad gave the man his name and the man checked him off the list. Dad went up the stairs to the landing, where he turned around, smiled and then waved to us before walking inside the plane.

We stayed in the car with my mom until the plane took off and I will always remember the car ride home. We were all quiet; there was nothing to be said while Mom was crying on the journey.

It was a solemn moment in our lives when Dad was leaving for a year and, to a child, time was the great unknown.

Chapter 5
Bead Beating

Before Dad went off to war, he set Mom up with a large voice recorder box, the size of a large travel case.

I remember my dad showing her how to use it, and before long, we received tapes shipped by Dad from overseas with the red, white and blue stripes around the edges of the package.

My mom would pull out the big case and set it up on the kitchen table, and she would set up the tapes for us to listen to the recording.

It was great to hear Dad's voice on the tape recorder. He would say hi to each of us by name and tell us a story. Mom would stop the tape when the tape got personal to Mom; you could tell by the tone of Dad's voice.

My mom would tell us to go out to play and she would continue to listen to the rest of the tape, then she would record her feedback.

Soon, Mom would call us back inside to the kitchen table, where we would talk back into the recorder.

We would tell Dad our stories, with Mom reminding us of events that had passed since our last recorded message to him.

Unknown to me at the time, my mom told me stories later in life of the family hardships while Dad was stationed in Vietnam. To my parents' credit, we never thought of or knew of the hardships that they went through in those days until being told of them later on.

Although Dad was not in the jungle like others fighting in the Vietnam War, I know that Dad worked at Da Nang Air Base in Vietnam, where he worked nights on the electronics of the airplanes that needed repairing.

He got into a lot of trouble with his superior officer on base for having a second job during the daytime, to pay my grandfather's loan back to him.

Dad was reprimanded and was passed over for a promotion due to not accepting the officer's orders that he could not have a second job during the daytime while fighting the war at night.

He said that he told the officer, who he had no respect for because he knew that he was stealing parts and sending them back home for profit, "Fuck off! What are you going to do? Send me home?"

My dad's military record was tarnished due to his need to provide for his family's hardships back home in Mississippi. Dad told me the story one day while we were working on his bathroom remodel.

I found out that Dad worked days at the Bank of America of all places, working with the GIs, helping them to fill out their life insurance policies and taking care of the cheques that bounced.

It turned out that they would write out cheques to the local business and the cheques would bounce due to lack of funds.

Our government would pay, unknown to the public, all the bounced cheques to any locals who came to the base to file a claim of a bounced cheque. Unbelievable, but it happened. Usually, either a service member had been killed in action or had just bluntly written bad cheques for services.

During the time my dad spent in Vietnam, some of the items he would send back in the mail included toy HO train cars and tracks, explaining to us on the tape recorder that he wanted us to save the pieces that he sent and that he would build us a train set that we could play with when he returned home.

It was something that my brother Charlie and I looked forward to when we received all the parts and pieces that he had sent to us by mail.

For many in my generation, we lived hearing about the stories of war on the news each night during the Vietnam years. Seeing the everyday turmoil of war with Walter Cronkite as the anchor man for the CBS Evening News.

It was an eye-opener, with my mother glued to the TV each night, seeing the horror of war and the sacrifices of our men fighting in Vietnam.

I remember one evening with Walter, that there was news of the air base where my father was stationed… It was under attack, with flashes of images of the attack shown on TV. My mother was visibly upset; she grabbed me and held onto me.

She suddenly stopped, walking into my parents' bedroom. I followed her and she shut the door behind us. She grabbed the rosary off the bedroom nightstand and started to pray with the rosary, telling me to stay with her.

As a child, my attention span was that of a gnat and I had never sat through a rosary prayer that long before. After the first stretch of the beads, I started to wonder when it was going to end.

My mother and I were one third of the way through the longest rosary bead session of my young life when I could hear her voice starting to become calmer. She probably saw the anguish in my face going through a major bead beating.

Then she snapped to when one of my younger brothers rescued me by yelling, "MOM?" as he walked through the front door of the trailer home. Thanks, bro…

Chapter 6
Their Actions Alone

After Dad was sent to Vietnam, unknown to my parents and to me at the time, the school that I was going to in first grade was still the school I was being bussed to in second grade—but with a twist.

I soon found out that I was to meet in the cafeteria with the other air force brats, only to then get put onto another bus and be sent to another school miles away.

Unknown to me that day, I was involved in the bussing of all-white children to an all-black school, with my counterparts from the all-black school being bussed to the all-white school in passing.

Mississippi had to meet the government requirements to receive any government funding to the Mississippi schools. With the local schools deciding to bus all the white children from the military families to the all-black schools.

My first memory of showing up to the all-black school was the military presence of the US Army National Guardsmen with M16s lined up in the parking area to the auditorium, where our bus pulled up to a stop.

Growing up in the air bases where we use to live, I was used to seeing military guards with guns at the main gates. So, seeing guards with guns was not unusual to me at the time.

What was unusual was the routine that followed for the next school year. Once there, we were removed from the bus and escorted directly into the school's auditorium, where we were all seated. You could soon hear the hustle all too familiar of children talking and moving through the halls going to their classes.

Once the bells rang and the classes started, we were all escorted to the classroom, where we would have a black schoolteacher waiting in our class. No black children were present in the classroom with us.

It was all too surreal from what we were used to in first grade. I remember having separate recesses from the black students, never interacting with any black children, only the adult black schoolteacher in front of us, who taught us all that school year.

Once the school day had ended, each day we would leave the class escorted separately to the auditorium, then would be escorted to our bus to take us back to the all-white school and then bussed back home.

As a child, being bussed, I knew that it was not normal; it was confining to me compared to the year before and I kept it to myself all these years.

I had other black children as friends that I played with that lived near the trailer park that same year, and that is what struck me to be the oddest thing as a child. I could not play with a black child in school, but when I got home, there were black children that I played with in the trailer park.

That was the most confusing thing for me at that age. How come I could play with black children at home in the trailer park, but when I went to school, I was shipped from an all-white school to an all-black school and could not even see or play with a black child at all, all day long.

We children of that time could only do what the men of power in Mississippi during that period would let us do under their control. They may not have even understood themselves that we as children played with no racist ideologies at home. For the air force brats, we learnt their side of racism from their actions alone.

Chapter 7
Vietnam War

The day finally came for Dad's homecoming from Vietnam in 1971. It was a great day. I remember getting in the car and heading out to the same airfield that Dad had left from to go to Vietnam the year before.

We pulled up to the same gated area in the car, and the plane flew in and taxied up to that familiar old three-foot high fence surrounding the airfield. The truck with the steps built on the back of the truck bed could not pull up fast enough to get my dad off the airplane. It turned out that Dad was the last one off the plane because he was the first one on it from wherever he had come from.

We ran out to the airfield with the other families, greeting all the Vets as they came off the airplane. It was a great moment in time, seeing all the people reunify as families again. It brings a tear to my eye when I think of that.

Dad finally showed up on top of the steps, just as we had started to wonder if he was even on the plane at all… Soon, he was down the steps and we were all over him, finally having our own reunion.

We all walked back to the car and Dad turned around and called me, "Charlie? What the heck?"

"Hey, Dad!" He was just kidding and tickled Charlie and me as we got into the back seat of the car. It was great to have him home again.

When we got home, Mom had made Dad his favourite meal. Back home at last to rest from the fatigue of his travels, starting with a home-cooked meal.

In conversations with Dad later on in life about the war, Dad said that he did not have as hard a time adjusting to coming home from the war as other guys who had been in 'the killing fields', as he put it.

He was on an air base far from the everyday grind of war, with a sniper taking pot-shots from time to time or a mortar shell attack on the base barracks, keeping them on guard and causing them to duck for cover in the worst case.

Dad did tell me of a death on the air base that had followed him home from the war that bothered him from time to time in his sleep. Dad was a US Marine before going to Vietnam in the US Air Force. One day, the air base was under mortar attack.

This was almost a daily occurrence at the base and Dad would just hit the deck wherever he was and make as small a target as possible for the mortars because he knew to do so as a marine.

He realised that mortars explode upward in a V-pattern, and the mortar has to be a direct hit to kill you. If you were standing up and a mortar hit near you, the odds were greater for you to die on the spot.

Dad had explained this to other bunk mates in his barracks and most listened to him, except for a few guys who would run for cover to 'a man-made mortar hut', as he called it, out front of each barracks.

One day, Dad was reading a book in his bunk when a mortar attack started. Dad explained that he just rolled under his bunk to make as small a target as possible and continued reading his book while others ran for the cover of the safety hut out front.

After the attack, there was word that one of his bunk mates had got it running outside for the cover of the mortar hut. It was an 18-year-old kid who had just been assigned to the barracks and had not got word of Dad's advice to his fellow bunk mates to just hit the deck and make as small a target as possible.

Dad said he went outside and the kid's body parts and chunks of him were all over the barracks next to theirs. The mortar was a direct hit next to him and the bottom half of his body from the hips down was still intact… but from his hips up, there was almost nothing left that was recognizable. His upper body was gone.

Dad and his bunk mates had the gruesome task of retrieving the kid's body parts and pulling chunks of his flesh up off of the barracks, helping to put him into a body bag. It bothered Dad all the rest of his life, he told me. That he felt guilty that he had not told the kid at the time to just roll up in place and make a small target.

He explained that whenever he saw that someone looked like the kid that had died, the events of that day would come back to haunt him the instant he saw the person, or sometimes later that night in his sleep.

Sometimes, he would see someone that looked like his scuba buddy from years earlier in the Pacific, who had died in a plane accident. The same thing happened to him with a twist, with the image of his friend in the same condition as the young kid that died in Vietnam.

Dad said life for the most part hit him square between the eyes when he got back home after the Vietnam War that day in Mississippi. Because all of us boys were all over him, making him quickly forget about the war in Vietnam. And so he settled back down into a new routine of family living.

A few days later, after Dad had got settled back in, we started to convert the two kids' bedrooms in the trailer home.

When Dad was in the Marine Corps on a ship and when he was not looking overboard, chumming for fish on the high seas… he slept on bunk beds stacked four rails high under the ship's deck.

Dad had decided to make his own version of the bunk beds in one of the two bedrooms. He put two 2x4s on each end of the wall, spanning with a galvanised 1" – 1/2" pole between them, making the beds four rails high.

Mom had sewn canvases together to slide the poles into pockets to support the bed mattress put on top of the canvas support. He installed them in an offset pattern, so we had a little head room as we got into each bed except for the top bunk—my bunk.

My bed was at the top of the heap closest to the ceiling, remembering that I had the warmest bed during the winter months ahead.

Dad had converted the other of the two bedrooms into a playroom. We started to build the train set from the pieces that Dad had sent to us from overseas in the playroom. He kept his promise to build the train set from the voice recordings sent from during the Vietnam War.

We also got our first family pet, a boxer puppy we named Missy. It was great having Dad home again. He was the missing piece of the puzzle and I soon felt the familiar peace that we had all longed for that returned once Dad was home again.

Working on the train set was bonding us back together again as a family, working and playing on the set, making up for time lost due to the Vietnam War.

Chapter 8
Unspoken Bond

Plans were being made for new adventures and soon felt the loss of Dad not being home vanish in the weeks that followed. The thought in the back of my head of being in charge of my brothers as Dad explained when he had left for Vietnam was soon lifted off my shoulders.

That same year, Dad was getting sent to Florida for temporary duty travel (TDY) to train other service personnel in electronics. The summer of '71 was going to be spent in Florida camping. Dad had rented a pop-up camper and we stayed in a campground near the base, as he was training others.

There was swimming and fishing in the nearby lakes, where we would fish for sunfish for supper and feed the guts, heads and bones to the alligators nearby the campgrounds.

The campground had a pool table in the camp's clubhouse, where we found out from the older kids that us smaller kids would get paid a penny to reach our smaller arms into the machine to trip the release mechanism for a cheaper game. We bought candy from the local store with the money made.

There were trips to Disney World and to Busch Gardens, where all the rides in the parks were ridden and with one of my memories of Dad getting hurt, when he stubbed his big toe, losing his toenail on one of the rides.

To us kids, it was the wildest thing to see a toenail missing in pain; I've never forgotten how it looked. It's one of the damnedest things you remember from childhood.

There was a trip to Miami Beach, where we stayed at a Howard Johnson Hotel, with a swimming pool on the roof! We found that truly amazing that a swimming pool could be on the roof of a building!

We also went to the Kennedy Space Centre, where we went through the museum and Dad had us pick out a memento to remember the trip by. I picked out a model to assemble of the lunar lander that landed on the moon.

We took a tour of the massive assembly tower, where we saw the rocket engine stage of Apollo 15 being loaded into the assembly tower. It was a massive engine assembly and I was so impressed with the size of everything involved.

We watched with amazement knowing that was the rocket engine that would be sending man to the moon. Our imaginations went wild knowing that we had seen part of Apollo 15's rocket.

We also saw the large platform crawler, with the massive tracks that took the assembled rocket to the staging area to be shot off to the moon. It was one of the greatest trips our family had experienced.

Soon our Florida family adventure was completed with the announcement that we had been transferred to Grissom Air Force Base in Bunker Hill, Indiana. I liked moving; it was an adventure when I was a kid.

Soon, we packed up the family wagon. The trailer home was being moved off the blocks and our home was on its way to Indiana.

We settled into our new trailer park in Bunker Hill; it was near open fields, hills and a creek. Soon we started to explore as only kids could do, with our imaginations running wild in the creeks and woods of Indiana.

My brothers and I for the next four years built forts in the woods and went fishing in the creeks, rivers and lakes nearby. We romped freely through the woods over the years, having adventure after adventure. I believe I truly found the freedom of my youth those next four years, with the confidence to make decisions on my own, no matter how bad they were.

Growing up with loving parents gave me my adventurous spirit to persist and take chances easily in life, no matter what life had to throw at us as a military family.

My brothers and I thrived in those years and built that unspoken bond between brothers that lasts to this day.

Chapter 9
Mom Was onto Us

Some of the adventures my brothers and I had as kids in the woods of Indiana were fun and for the most part harmless, but not all. A few ill adventures must be told.

One early morning, I went down to the creek near our home, only to run across one of the craziest kids in the trailer park—David.

David had a raccoon cornered with two long sticks, one in each hand. He was keeping the raccoon at bay in the bend of the creek, with a steep short cliff behind the creature.

He said, "Hey, you're just in time to help me catch this raccoon!" It seemed like the right thing to do at the time. Heck, half of the battle was already under way and the raccoon looked tired to me.

So, David handed me both sticks and I continued keeping the raccoon at bay. We had one pissed off raccoon in a corner and it was not having as much fun as we were.

David, who had started the whole adventure, decided to take the shoestrings off his shoes and create a lasso with which to catch the raccoon. With the shoestring lasso in hand, he jumped up on top of the short cliff behind the raccoon, lying on his stomach and leaning over, missing with the first attempt to hit the raccoon with the lasso.

The raccoon went ballistic! The raccoon found a burst of energy and when David tried to lasso it the second time, the raccoon jumped up and bit David in the forearm.

I was amazed at the feat the raccoon had just pulled off and then the raccoon turned towards me. We looked at each other and the raccoon seized the moment and ran towards me in a fit of rage, as I started diving away from the raccoon with both sticks still in hand.

I had a newfound respect for wildlife after that adventure. David had to go to the doctor's and I found out later that he had to get rabies shots in the gut with a six-inch needle because they could not find the raccoon to find out if it had rabies or not.

So, he had to receive the rabies shots every week for some time just in case the raccoon did have rabies. Ouch, it hurts just thinking about it.

Another fine adventure my brother Charlie and I had with David one hot summer day was when we were on top of a dry grassy field overlooking the trailer park and we decided to play a game we invented called 'on top of old smoky', our favourite folk song of the day and the name seemed appropriate with what we were doing that day.

The way the game went was that David would light a match and throw it in the weeds on the ground as Charlie and I would stomp out the fire whilst the smoke was rising. Soon, we got more daring. David would light the match, and we would let the fire get a little more out of control and then stomp it out.

After two successful attempts, we decided together as a group to let the next game of 'on top of old smoky' go a little further on. David lit the match and threw it into the weeds, giving it some time to spread out. We were stomping away to put the fire out when a gust of wind came up out of nowhere and took the fire to another level. Suddenly, the fire was out of control!

We all looked at each other and then ran down the hill, across the creek and to our bicycles that we had left at the base of the wooded hills.

We found that some other kids were involved in a kickball game that was in progress and we joined in on the game.

Soon, one of the kids we were playing with said, "Hey, look! There's a fire on the hill!" David, Charlie and I looked as dumbfounded as we could at the time and joined in to watch, as the fire department showed up to put the fire out.

Once the fire department had put out the fire and completed their fire investigation, they figured it was kids from the neighbourhood playing with matches who had started the fire.

The fire department got us kids together to find out who the culprits were and because we all had such good alibis with the other kids playing kickball, we were deemed not under suspicion by the fire department. But Mom was onto us.

Now, Mom had known that we were playing with David in the woods nearby… where the hill was on fire. She did not have to ask us who had started the fire because she had a mother's intuition about our friend David.

We had skated the charges with the fire inspector, only to have Mom with her motherly intuitions ask a few more questions later. The questions only a mother could ask, as if they have their eyes at the back of their heads.

Knowing that Mom watched *Columbo* with Dad weekly… Mom started to ask the tough questions and we were under interrogation.

"If you were playing kickball, why are your shoes wet and charred with black soot?"

Mom was onto us; we had nothing on her, and how did the fire investigator miss that one?

We were in awe. Without another word said, Mom had found her reason to have David banned for life, no questions asked.

Chapter 10
Between Brothers

Rural Indiana was a great place to live. I went to Mead Elementary School in Indiana from third grade through to fifth grade, where some of the stories from the last chapter were soon to be our legacy at our school.

Everyone knew of the Deatherage brothers, that we were trouble and to stay clear. Our legacy only grew with the stories about us being told by David.

My brother and I kept our mouths shut and tried to keep out of trouble for the most part, until our legacy of being troublemakers exploded with our next ill adventure.

The next big ill adventure that comes to mind after David was banned for life was when my brother Charlie and I were at a Boy Scouts jamboree with our Boy Scout troop. I will not say what state it was in to protect the guilty parties.

The guys from our troop were simple country kids from the sticks with nothing but mischief in mind. We had our typical firecracker fights and BB gun fights, shooting at each other. But when whoever crossed our path from another troop, they got it good with whatever we were into at that time.

We were a pack of wolves together as a troop and we were the troop that got in trouble the most from the scout master in charge of the jamboree that weekend.

In the middle of the night, we would pull the tent stakes out of the scout master's tent along with other tents, threw firecrackers in their fires until someone woke up and found their tents deflated—stuff like that. Just a fun-loving bunch of country boys.

We got the first looks the next morning from the scout master, who pointed his finger in our troop's direction with only unknown guilty accusations, because we did not get caught doing the deeds. But our tents were the only ones left standing in the morning untouched.

My brother Charlie and I were looking for firewood that same day by ourselves when we ran across a dead tree deep in the woods but not too far from our camp.

We had our family axe and started taking turns chopping a notch into the tree, to fell the dead tree for firewood.

After some time chopping away at the tree, it started to fall over. What we did not know at the time was that there were green-coloured power lines in the woods that we had not seen. Who puts green power lines in the damn forest?

The heavy tree fell across both power lines midspan between the power poles. Only a lineman could explain what would happen next.

The closest power pole transformer exploded immediately! *BOOM!* The transformer was close by, so it made the largest explosion as it went off. Then we heard every transformer for miles away starting to explode! *BOOM! BOOM! Boom! Boom! Boom! Boom*, with other transformers exploding in the distance, until we could not hear them exploding anymore. Charlie and I were used to this routine by now; we looked at each other and we ran off back to the camp, looking as dumbfounded as we could.

In stealth mode, we snuck back into camp as we got closer, with sticks in our hands from our firewood expedition so as not to rouse any suspicions.

The scouts from the other troops were asking, "Did you guys hear those explosions? What was that? Hey, the power's out at the main store!"

Our response was, "Oh, really?"

The fire department and local utility company later found out that our firewood tree was the problem and there were no beavers in the local area.

The power company soon put two and two together that it must have been some kids chopping down the tree that caused the whole incident from the nearby Boy Scout jamboree.

They informed the jamboree scout master in charge to get all us scouts together; there must have been 200 of us gathered around.

He explained that whoever had cut the tree down was damn lucky to be alive and wanted to know who the culprits were and to come forward on their oath of honour to confess their mistake in judgment.

All the kids were just looking at one another to see which sap sucker had done the dirty deed, as well as Charlie and myself in stealth mode, looking around too for the culprits.

Luckily, David was not with us; they would have smelt him out in a hot minute, the troublemaker that he was. He probably would have proudly admitted it!

Luckily, it was just between Charlie and me; only brothers in blood could keep this type of a secret between each other.

When we had walked back into the campsite hours before, we had sworn secrecy to the firewood adventure until our dying days.

Being raised Catholics, knowing we could go to confession for our sins, we would have opted for that route to save our parents the expense of the hefty bill that was sure to come with such an unspoken dastardly deed.

To go to confession the next Sunday and hope that Walter Cronkite did not pick up on the story that half of the state we were in had lost its power near to the Boy Scouts Jamboree. Our parents would have caught on to that for sure!

Only years later did we tell our parents—as we all do, right? Only after the statute of limitations had expired to adulthood could our childhood ill adventures be told, from years of secrecy between brothers.

Chapter 11
First School Dance

When I started sixth grade, I was moved to the new middle school in the area. The school we went to was huge compared to the schools that I'd been to in the past.

Maconaquah Junior High School in Bunker Hill, Indiana, was a new school in the area at that time. It even had its own auditorium and planetarium buildings.

To a country bumpkin like me, it was overwhelming and my reputation from Mead Elementary was soon left behind. David's family moved from the area to another base and I had a new fresh start with a clean slate at Maconaquah.

My parents had encouraged me to get into music. So, I picked out an alto saxophone in a Sears, Roebuck and Company catalogue. My parents ordered it and soon picked it up at the local Sears' store before school started up that year.

I was enrolled in music class at Maconaquah, learning scales and practicing them at home. I enjoyed the saxophone and in class we were pitted against one another to become first chair, second chair, and so on, to encourage us to get better in music class.

It furthered my adventurous spirit to persist and thrive to become bolder and to fight to become better at the alto saxophone.

The one thing that I did not become better at was soon to be known by all at school. It was the first year I was involved in a school dance.

I remember it being a big deal at school in the hallways… There were banners made by girls, of course, about going to the dance after school in the gymnasium. So, I was encouraged by my mom to go to the dance as a curious bystander… to see what this school dance was going to be all about.

My mom had spun her web to see how the first of her four boys would react to his first school dance. Kids were out dancing, but I had no idea how to dance… I'd never even seen dancing… except for on the Lawrence Welk show on TV, but where were the bubbles? Where were the band and singers?

There was no sissy faction in the Deatherage household… I had no sisters, only brothers, and we just beat each other up for entertainment. This was a whole new ball game—holding hands, getting close to girls, dancing!

It had never entered my mind to even think of girls in a close way. But I'm sure girls thought of us boys… holding hands of all things, dancing… I'm sure the girls looked at all of this in a whole different way.

So, I backed myself into a corner with all the other guys that got sap suckered into the event by their mothers, drinking punch, listening to the rock music of the early '70s and acting too cool for school.

I did dance one time on the dance floor… Some of us were too shy to ask girls to dance… when towards the end of the dance, a girl I recognised from my music class came up to me to ask me to dance a slow dance.

I had watched other slow dancing being done that same night and that had looked like the time to dance if there was going to be any time to dance for me.

Any clodhopper could do that, I remember thinking.

The song that we slow danced to was *Mandy* by Barry Manilow. I remember thinking after the song was over… for those who know the song… that I was glad that it was over… It had seemed like the song went on and on and on.

This was just starting to feel like the bead beating I had taken from Mom when Dad was in Vietnam. I don't remember the name of the girl that I danced with, but I'm sure that she remembers my name, what the date was, what time it was and what I was wearing, shoe colour, etc. After the dance, she kissed me on the cheek and ran away.

Apparently, my attention span had not changed. I found out about myself that I still had the attention span of a gnat, when it came to the rosary and now girls. After the dance, I tried to steer clear from them both, knowing that a dance was a whole other world compared to the rough and tumble world that I had come from with three brothers in the backwoods of Indiana.

Looking back, I think it was awkward to me because I was all boy. I came from the sticks, having played in the creeks, mud, and the muck. Building forts in the woods, climbing trees, fighting wild animals with sticks, us boys shooting BB guns at each other, throwing firecrackers at guys, pulling stakes out from tents, letting the air out of them and blowing up countywide electrical grids.

I do remember looking at the only girl that I knew at the time… my mother… in a whole new way. She had only done what any sneaky mom would do to a child with only boys as siblings.

I'm sure that she smiles about the day her oldest son went to his first school dance, setting me up like an experiment for all the other brothers to follow in her spun web.

Soon, I was back to normal. Back to my rough and tumble ways, beating up my brothers… surly from the traumatic experience of my first school dance.

Chapter 12
Turn the Page

It was not long after the dance that my dad announced that he was getting ready to retire from the air force that year and that he was going to retire us all to McClellan Air Force Base in Sacramento, California.

I was a little bummed out because Bunker Hill, Indiana, was the first place where I could remember growing up, somewhere all of us brothers had truly been able to call home for a time.

But once I had told our friends that we were moving to California, it eased a little. We heard that California it was! It has everything! Hollywood, beaches, the Pacific Ocean, the Sierra Mountains, surfing, snow skiing! Gold in the hills! Wow, this could be another adventure in the making.

Hey, this was starting to sound a whole lot better as more friends found out and we talked about the move to California.

Before we moved, we went to go and visit our grandparents' home in Knoxville, Tennessee. Our grandparents' home was always our home base throughout my youth growing up as an air force brat.

No matter where we were stationed, my grandparents' home on Gary Road in Knoxville, Tennessee was the focal point of the whole Deatherage clan and we visited there every year.

Grandpa also made some of the best damn BBQ ribs that could only be made with a secret family recipe from East Tennessee.

Now, I knew as a child that Grandpa had kept a clear liquidly substance in a Mason jar in the cellar to sip on and to 'clean the rust off the tools', as he put it, chuckling.

He also had cases and cases of Mason jars all around that were all empty, chuckling a little more. Was my grandpa a bootlegger? For as long as I had known, there had always been empty cases of Mason jars…

Every time we visited Grandpa, he had a special jar set aside for us grandchildren to sip on when we visited; we were sworn to secrecy that we could not tell Mom or Nana of the Mason jars in the cellar.

Dad, of course, was in on the secret of the White Lightning Mason jars in the basement.

We had a great family visit as always, with our aunts and uncles telling family stories untold. With us kids hanging around with our cousins, playing rook, sipping iced tea and other drinks from the cellar when our parents were not looking, under Grandpa's supervision, of course.

Our cousins, uncles and aunts on my dad's side of the family would be missed and we knew that, with moving to California, we would not see them as much as we used to growing up.

Soon, in the early summer of 1976, my dad transferred his papers to retire in California. The trailer home was being moved off the blocks once again and our home was on its way to California. California, here we come!

By now, I had travelled extensively in my young life up to this point and we were used to a road trip. As usual, Dad had the trip planned down to every detailed stop that he could think of on the way.

The largest ball of twine, a couple of Pony Express stops for the old mail routes of the Pony Express days, a couple of old cavalry forts, the stuffed horse of Roy Rogers, my dad's childhood idol.

Dad had put out the request to review the map of the trip and pick out any locations that we would be interested to stop at on the way.

Of course, my only smart-ass request as the older brother was to remind Dad that he was banned from making toast on the great overland trip; to make sure that the ban on Dad making toast still stood, protecting my younger siblings from the experience that was charred in my memory.

It was agreed; now, apart from burnt toast, Dad knew how to make a great, adventurous road trip.

The Grand Canyon was one of the greatest memories and we spent a week there exploring.

It was an amazing adventure hiking down the canyon and viewing the overlooks and monuments in the area at different times of the day. The colours of the canyon walls were amazing to see.

We also saw vultures flying overhead, feeding on a carcass down the side of the canyon some distance away. For us boys, that was a great treat seeing the activity of everyday nature at work.

We had soon set up camp at the park and before long had a new neighbour at the campsite who was a native American from the area. He was camping by himself next to our campsite. He told us that he had just got out of the army and he was unwinding before going home. The Vietnam War had ended.

He visited with us, showing us how he had played with a type of weed when he was a kid that when shaped in the correct way, you could shoot the weed at your brother like it was a bow and arrow.

While my brothers and I played with our newfound toy, I could see the young man talking with my dad and the conversation turned to some of their experiences in Vietnam.

Dad was back from the war and had been home for some time by then, but the young man seemed to want to talk to my dad in private about it.

You could see the anguish in the young man's face and that he wanted to talk to my father alone.

My dad shooed us off to get away, and soon he and my dad walked away in conversation. You could tell the young man was crying as they walked away.

Whatever the conversation was about, you could tell the young man felt better after a while and soon joined us for dinner in camp that night.

I never asked my dad what their talk had been about, but I came away thinking that whatever my dad had said to him must have made sense to the young man.

Everyone needs to talk to someone once in a while. When you feel comfortable talking to them, then suddenly the feelings will just pour out like they did for that young man.

The next morning, we woke up and found our new native American friend had left his campsite overnight, never to be seen again. I hope he was able to turn the page on what was bothering him.

Chapter 13
Mason Jar Half-Full

That same morning, Dad announced that we were leaving the Grand Canyon and that we were going off to see the London Bridge in the middle of the desert in Lake Havasu, Arizona... So, we packed up the family wagon and off we went.

Once we got there, we set up camp and set off to see the bridge. It was the craziest thing you could ever see! The bridge had been taken apart in London, England, stone by stone, numbered and then shipped back to Lake Havasu to be reassembled.

The London Bridge in the middle of the desert... Wow! There was nothing else around it, literally... We had a picnic near the bridge and walked around the structure in awe.

That evening, we settled into camp and started up a fire outside the tent; it had been a long day and we were all tired, hitting the sack early.

During the middle of that night, we were all awoken by my mother screaming... Not a regular scream, but a blood-curdling scream!

We had all woken up with thoughts of the worst possible scenarios you could have imagined in the pitch dark! The tent was in an uproar... with us all experiencing something jumping on us… Adding to the confusion was all of us screaming, "It's over here!!!"… "Now, now it's on me!!!"

From one of my brothers yelling, "Now it's on me!!!"

Another brother yelled, "Argh, what was it?" All of a sudden it was on ME.

"Argh!!!!"… We were all under attack!

Dad finally got to the lantern and lit it… only to find out that the monster in the tent was a small field mouse that had gotten inside the tent and had keeled over from the excitement that it had caused. The poor mouse was scared to death by the Deatherage family…

My dad picked up the mouse to find out that the tent flap had been left open by one of us kids going outside to go pee.

Dad yelled, "Now you know why it is important to close the damn tent flap all the way. What if that had been a rattlesnake?! Close the damn tent flap when you come back inside, damn it!" We all went back to bed, eventually all laughing ourselves to sleep…

We all woke up the next day and went to go outside that morning only to see that the small field mouse, being crawled over by ants, had completed its cycle of life…

We packed up the tent with excitement, knowing that we were off to the next stop on our overland trip. To visit the home of Uncle Med and Aunt Frankie, who were stationed at Nellis Air Force Base in Las Vegas, Nevada.

Uncle Med was a colonel in the Air Force and was a squadron commander, who flew F-4 Phantoms in the Vietnam War and in Europe during the Cold War.

To us kids, Uncle Med was the cool uncle, and he looked the part of a fighter pilot. He was a lean man who stood six feet, four inches tall and had a cool demeanour. Most of the times I had seen him, he had been wearing the military jumpsuit that the fighter pilots wore, sporting aviator sunglasses.

We were visiting my aunt and uncle when I walked out into the garage, where my dad and Uncle Med were hanging out, and I noticed a familiar Mason jar on the bench counter.

"Hey, that looks like some of Grandpa's White Lightning, Dad. How did that get out here?"

Dad and Uncle Med said, "Hey, well look at it there!" With me not knowing that they had already been sipping on it, they cracked open the jar and took a few more sips whilst laughing, letting me have a sip, too.

Now there were a lot of great stories told about Uncle Med. Uncle Med was raised in the Smoky Mountains in East Tennessee, where he courted my aunt and married her. I remember them visiting my parents in South Dakota when I was a kid and they were as close to me as an uncle and aunt could be to a nephew of 12 years of age.

So, in confidence, my dad and Uncle Med, with the Mason jar half full, decided to tell me a story about Uncle Med and Grandpa that no one else could know about in the family.

It was top secret at the time, but the statute of limitations has passed… so now the story can be told…

Chapter 14
Stays in Vegas

The story goes that there was a top-secret mission that my uncle flew twice a year to the Pentagon from Nellis Air Force Base, where he had to report to his commanders at the Pentagon about his command at Nellis Air Force Base. "An evaluation of his squadron of a sort," as Uncle Med put it.

Uncle Med would file a flight plan to fly his F-4 Phantom for military manoeuvers into the Knoxville Airport in East Tennessee for some 'touch and go' landings.

The term 'touch and go' was a military term meaning to land and take off in an all-in-one motion without stopping... only to fly off again.

The name for this military manoeuver was the term used to the flight tower in case the local press got wise to the unusual military action in the area.

If somebody asked why there was a F-4 Phantom flying in and out of the Knoxville Airport, there was the answer of, "Oh, they were doing touch and goes, practicing military manoeuvers."

Uncle Med would call my grandpa in Tennessee from Las Vegas and set up an ETA, 'estimated time of arrival', to meet up with Grandpa...

My grandpa would work around the house, waiting for the signal until it arrived. The signal was for Uncle Med to buzz my grandfather's house with the F-4 Phantom… Quite the signal…

The whole neighbourhood knew of the signal as a wave from Uncle Med as he flew over from time to time. I could just hear my grandpa's neighbours now… "WHAT THE… oh… that must be Medford with his airplane waving 'Hey y'all.'"

Once Grandpa got the signal… he would get in his car and drive out to the airport that was ten minutes from the house… while Uncle Med buzzed a few other hillbilly friends in the hills nearby to say, "Hey y'all," to them.

Once the time was up after Grandpa's signal to leave the house, Uncle Med would do a couple of touch and go landings for the airport tower's excitement until Grandpa would get to the airport to see the military event as a curious bystander.

My uncle would fly in for the final touch and go… only to land the F-4 Phantom… taxiing over the three-foot high fence, where my grandpa was parked nearby. Grandpa would hop over the three-foot high fence and walk up to the parked F-4 fighter plane with the cases of Mason jars filled with White Lightning…

Uncle Med explained that he had had his crew attach an empty camera pod to the plane's under wing rail, where the sidewinder's missiles were normally attached.

It was rigged so that Grandpa could use a large Phillips-head screwdriver to open the camera pod doors up by removing the screws on each side door.

After placing the cases of White Lightning onto the pre-manufactured wooden slots built into the camera pod, he would bungee cord down the lid to the wooden boxes. When Grandpa was done screwing the camera pod doors back on, he would give Uncle Med the thumbs-up.

Uncle Med would salute Grandpa to make it look official and all, then Grandpa would walk back to hop over the fence. After that Uncle Med would taxi out to take off, finishing the 'go' part of the touch and go manoeuver.

It was all very official-looking… carried out with the upmost military precision. Uncle Med and my grandfather had cooked up the top-secret mission to the Pentagon on my grandfather's front porch while having a BBQ and sipping on White Lightning one weekend.

After our visit, while we were leaving Las Vegas, the popular saying of today rang true: "What happens in Vegas stays in Vegas!"

Chapter 15
Overland Trail

After leaving Las Vegas, we drove straight to California to dip our toes in the Pacific Ocean and to find a campsite nearby.

The plan was to visit my mother's side of the family in California for the first time in our young lives and then start up to Sacramento to meet up at the trailer home and set up our homestead.

After setting up camp, it was planned to visit Papa for the first time in our lives that evening.

We soon got to the apartment and greeted Papa with a big hug, with our attention being drawn to a large platter of food in the centre of his dining table.

Papa was a chef and knew how to set up a table with food, and the feed bags were on. He said in his broken Greek, "Eat! Eat!"

We were on that table of food like vultures over a carcass, just as we had seen in the desert only days before, at the Grand Canyon in Arizona.

Before long, there were only bones left over and our attention went to the other guest in the home.

Papa was sitting back with a large smile on his face while enjoying the feeding frenzy on display.

We also met for the first time our aunt Henny and her husband, whose name escapes me but who I remember because he only had one leg.

Of course, with four curious boys around, it did not take long for us to ask the inevitable questions. "Hey, how did you lose the leg? Did you lose it in battle?"

With Mom saying, "Hey! That's not polite!"

He got a kick out of the questions because he knew they were coming up, what with all four boys eyeballing his missing leg while eating in a frenzied silence.

He and Papa had a great laugh, knowing beforehand that his missing leg would eventually come up in conversation. But they probably did not figure on it being so soon.

Aunt Henny's husband explained how he had lost his leg in a tractor accident while farming as a kid, when he was about our age. With the explanation at hand and with our attention span being that of gnats, we soon became restless due to the fact that we were overland explorers.

Then we were off exploring the rest of the apartment, becoming bored quickly and wanting to go outside.

Next, it was off to our campsite with Papa, who stayed the night with us camping. We talked with Papa that night by our campfire, telling him about our adventures and him telling us stories about his adventures coming to America, teaching us words in Greek. It was a lot of fun and we all had a great time.

The next morning, we packed up the tent and we were off to a picnic that was planned to see our uncle Leon in Santa Barbara, with his kids at a park near his home. My uncle's children were older and most were living on their own by that point.

We all got together and soon food was the center of attention again, as family members started to show up.

It was fun seeing our new-found cousins for the first time, showing up one at a time at the park. One pulled up on a Harley-Davidson motorcycle, another in a souped-up Chevy Camaro, coming to a screeching halt at the park. *Cool!*

They were full of life, laughing and kidding with Mom and Dad, going over old stories and photos of when they were kids. They had known Mom and Dad before they'd got married and it was 12 years since they'd all seen each other last.

It was fun and we had a great visit. After the picnic, we were on the road again. On to Sacramento and to McClellan Air Force Base to meet up at our trailer home.

Once we got to Sacramento, we set up camp in West Sacramento at a Kampgrounds of America (KOA) campground along the delta. Dad had gone to the base to check in his retirement papers and to get them in order, and to find out where the mobile trailer home was located.

Dad soon got back to the campground to tell us that our trailer home was in Nevada, and that the frame of the trailer was bent from the load it was carrying. That it was sitting in a tractor trailer parking area, somewhere in Reno, Nevada.

The California Highway patrol (CHP) would not let the trailer over the California State Line until it was fixed and the contents of the trailer removed, due to the state's weight limits to drive through the Sierra Mountains on Highway 80.

We would have to go and unload the trailer to lighten up the load and arrange for the trailer home to be repaired, then arrange for another tractor trailer truck to pick up the trailer once repaired.

Dad rented a U-Haul trailer and took us boys up to the trailer to help unload it. We found the trailer and we all saw the damage for the first time.

The trailer's frame was bent, as if the tractor trailer driver had gone over a speed bump going over a hundred miles an hour, my dad explained.

My imagination went wild. Wow! The trailer must have been flying in the air, only to come down and bend the frame at the axel to the rear of the home. It looked like the ass end of the trailer was dragging on the ground.

Dad went into a repair shop to find out how much it was going to cost to fix the trailer and to get it back on the road again. It was going to take weeks to get the repairs made, because the shop was too busy working on other tractor trailers.

We unloaded the contents of our mobile home trailer into the U-Haul and went back to the campsite to tell Mom the bad news. The campground was going to be home for a while.

We were homeless for the first time in our lives but Dad did not look at it that way. He told us that we were not homeless, that we were still on our overland adventure and that this was what the pioneers went through back in the Gold Rush days!

Dad had made a great point and there was a history lesson to be learnt there as well. Dad had us busy scavenging as the overland pioneers had done in the Gold Rush days.

We were all over the area like Jedediah Smith, fishing in the delta for food and exploring the Sacramento River Delta with our imaginations running wild.

Looking back, Dad had made our overland camp into an adventure of a lifetime. He turned a hardship monument on the overland trail into a fun summertime break along the trail.

He showed us that no matter what happens in your life, you are the only one who can fix it and you had better fix it quickly or you're going to starve to death on life's great adventure.

Chapter 16
Dedicated Service

Soon, word came that the trailer home had been repaired in Reno. Dad had already scouted out a lot at a trailer park nearby for the trailer once it was fixed and had it moved to our new temporary home.

The trailer park that Dad picked out was near Magpie Creek in North Highlands. There was a motorcycle track in the nearby fields for Dad to ride his bike around.

It was going to be a temporary location, my dad explained, because Mom and Dad were in the market for buying a new home. It was going to be about a year for our family's California official settlement plan to take effect on a new homestead.

It was the summer of 'the spirit of 76', and our country's bicentennial was being celebrated. On the 4th of July, we all went to the state fairgrounds in Sacramento to watch the fireworks that night. What a great way to celebrate our new beginning in California!

Our great overland adventure had officially come to a close. We had completed our trip from Indiana to California just as the settlers did over 126 years earlier.

I looked back thinking about our family trip and what a great adventure it had been, with all the great memories!

My parents were now back in California, where it had all started for them, and with a new plan and a new beginning to the next chapter in their lives, just as they had planned years before.

They had come full circle to their retirement and we had all turned the page on our military lifestyle, and what a great adventure it was. A chance of a lifetime. Happy 200th birthday, America!

Soon we were registered for school; I was going on 13 years old at the time of the great overland adventure days. Soon, I had started my last year of junior high school, at Foothill Junior High School in North Highlands, California.

I was pleasantly surprised in my first year of going to school in California to find out that the school I was going to was an open-air campus because, hey man... we were in California. The weather was great!

The weather was nothing like back east in the places we had been stationed. We went through lightning storms, humidity, tornadoes, freezing ice storms, whiteout snow conditions that covered your home, and oh yes, Hurricane Camille with burnt toast the next day.

It was odd for me at first and it took a while to get used to the open-air campus, but there was a newfound freedom in this and California started to agree with me.

You could walk out to the open hallways and cross the open grassy areas between the classes in the sunshine.

I thought, *Hey, this California is some kind of cool place...*

At the time, there were no fences surrounding the schools and if you wanted to, you could walk wherever you wanted to as long as you made it back to class on time.

Our P.E. classes were interesting as well. The whole school would get together for P.E. with both the boys and girls gathered in the same instruction area to start exercises as one group.

The instructors were like military drill instructors. There was the girls' section and the boys' section. All were in line in the schoolyard outside and we would all take roll-call.

The boys' roll-call included having to snap our mandatory jockstrap to show that we were wearing them, as the girls giggled.

After roll-call and a snap, we were off to our separate instructors, with the girls' instructors taking them around the surrounding fields and the boys doing the same under a different instructor.

Kids even went off campus to the surrounding fields near the high school to eat their lunches at lunchtime, like having a picnic.

I was amazed to see kids feeding seagulls in the fields, because I had thought that seagulls were an ocean bird and wondered what they were doing so far inland.

They are a smart, opportunistic bird, only showing up at feeding time like vultures and are unafraid to sneak up on some poor sap sucker to steal their lunch right from under them from time to time.

We got a good laugh at that and the fact that if you were overfeeding a group of seagulls, eventually there would be 20 birds around someone fighting for food, with the odds that one of the seagulls would poop on some kid within the vicinity of the feeding frenzy.

It happened almost every time there was a feeding frenzy and I would just sit back undercover and watch for someone to get splattered with what looked like yogurt all over a six-inch perimeter of their body.

It became a new sport for me at lunchtime to gather some of my friends and say, "Hey, watch this. One of these gulls is going to poop on some kid soon." It happened almost every time.

California was a new beginning. My dad had always taught us to think outside of the box and California was the greatest playground to do just that with its great, vast open spaces.

Soon we settled into a new routine in our temporary California homestead. Dad had bought a *Beach Boys* album for us kids and soon we were California dreaming and surfing on our skateboards all over the driveways and back roads and parks.

We started exploring the Pacific Ocean and the Sierra Mountains that year, dreaming of the California gold we had heard about from Dad on the great overland adventure.

Soon, Mom and Dad found their dream home after all the years of travel and their dedicated service to our country.

Dad always picked a good location for us kids to be stationed growing up as air force brats. The main rule of thumb was that our new home needed to be near a creek, river, or lake, and he found all three nearby to our new home.

We had finally settled into our California dream home as Dad had promised after the great overland move out west.

It was a great homestead find and looking back, my parents had turned the page on their well-deserved retirement in the town of Citrus Heights, California.

Chapter 17
Fishing Adventures

From our home we would get on our bicycles and ride 20 to 30 minutes in any direction and you could be fishing with a good buddy or doing whatever, depending on what caught your interest along the way.

Our nearest ride to a fishing hole was north, down a rocky trail that today is known as Rocky Ridge Drive in Roseville, California.

It was properly named with the rock trails that bounced our bicycles all over the trail and occasionally claimed a victim by throwing them off of the beaten path into a batch of star thistles, a nasty weed with pointy thorns on them that grows in large bundles in California. It was a great laugh when it happened to someone else… but when it happened to you, it hurt like hell and you were not the one laughing.

Our fishing destination along the Rocky Ridge trail was a creek called Miners Ravine. This area is where the gold miners dug into the sides of the hills near Roseville, California, during the Gold Rush days.

It was a great place to explore when we were kids. We explored the abandoned caves along the creek and fished for trout, making day camp along the creek or in one of the many abandoned caves to set up a campfire, eating the trout right off of a stick for lunch.

There were locations if you went far enough back into a nearby ranch, where there were deep narrow valleys with caves, with old beam supports and with wooden doors into the caves. There were even candle droppings built up on ledges inside the caves where gold miners worked and lived.

One of the greatest things about fishing in Miners Ravine in the early fall were the salmon runs. My friends and I would ride our bikes down to the creek, where we would fish for salmon in the shallow areas of the creek.

One day, my buddy—who had his baseball bat with him—decided to whack one on the head as it landed on the shore next to him.

We learnt from the school of hard knocks that some of the salmon were too big to whack. They were too big to put on the bike ape handlebars and they would drag on the ground, so we learnt to go for the smaller, mid-size ones.

We would fill the ape handlebars of our bicycles with salmon and would ride to my buddy's home and smoke the salmon that we had fished—or 'whacked for' as we liked to call it…

Legal side note: We were kids of the '70s… There were no laws known to kids not to whack salmon with bats at the time and I recommend not to do this back home in Citrus Heights today.

On other fishing expeditions 20 minutes to the south, we would ride our bikes along Fair Oaks Boulevard to Winding Way and through the town of Old Fair Oaks.

Our gateway to our fishing paradise was the crossing over the American River, on an old steel and wooden-planked bridge that was no longer in use for cars. We rode our bikes over to our fishing holes and sometimes if you were not careful, your bicycle tire would get caught in the wooden planks and you would have to pull your tire out of the rut you had gotten stuck in.

Most of the time on our southern trips we would fish with a fishing pole, believe it or not… right off the banks. We would only get a couple of fish with the poles, but we were kids and got bored from the spoils from the whacking expeditions up north at Miners Ravine.

There were only a few areas along the American River where we could get our whacks in with a baseball bat and we had to ride further upriver, which made for a longer fishing day. On the next weekend, we decided we would leave the fishing poles at home and play ball.

On the following expeditions we knocked it out of the park; my buddy and I filled the ape bars with fish and started on our way back home.

Little did I know that I was going to have my first business experience on this trip on the way back, which sparked a string of very unusual small business adventures to come in my later teenage years.

I got a flat front tire in Old Fair Oaks, near the town square park. The local stores' alleyways in the area were still unpaved, with gravel spilling out into the main paved roadways, and I happened to run over a sharp rock on the road.

Damn the luck! I did not have the money or the means on the road to fix my flat tire when an old man approached me to see if he could help with the flat. Wow! "Some catch you guys got there," he said, as the fish were stacked on our handlebars, almost overflowing.

"If you did not have such a big load, then you might not have gotten a flat," he commented, as he smiled jokingly. There was a filling station close by and the old man offered to pay five bucks for one of the fish so that I could get my tire fixed.

"Cool! Thanks, Mr!"

He said, "Any time, and next time you come back from one of your fishing expeditions, make sure you stop by my house over there and I'll help you lighten the load off of those handlebars, young man."

"OK, you got it! Thanks again for your help!"

We went to the filling station to get my tire fixed when the guy fixing my flat tire offered me ten bucks for the big salmon on the handlebars. "Heck ya, you got it."

We were rolling in dough, man, and had doubled our money from the last sale! We were not even out the filling station parking lot when a guy pulled up for gas and wanted to buy another fish! Wow! Cha-ching! This was a whole other way to make dough and fast.

I was 13 years old when I got the itch to start making cash that late fall. I was only disappointed to learn the following week that the fish had started to thin out from the end of the salmon run. Afterwards, I went to go buy taller ape handlebars for my bike to carry more fish.

I learnt at a young age that money can come and go with the market and it was a valuable lesson learnt. I needed to plan my investments in advance before spending cash on larger unusable ape handlebars. They were still cool anyway.

Chapter 18
Price of Freedom

In my early teenage years, Citrus Heights was still a rural area north of Sacramento, bordering the Placer County line.

There were still a lot of orchards and farmland in the surrounding areas and it was not unusual to smell skunks, and see coyotes, foxes, raccoons, or deer along Cripple Creek, behind our family home off of Fair Oaks Boulevard.

Citrus Heights is centrally located in Northern California, my dad explained. You could go in any direction in one hour and be at the ocean beaches basking in the sun one weekend, listening to the waves crashing in on the shoreline. Then the next weekend go backpacking, camping, hunting and fishing in the Sierra Mountains.

For kids growing up in a family whose parents were active with their children and took us on adventures all our lives, Citrus Heights was the amazing hub for all types of family adventures.

When we were not on a weekend adventure out of town, we could go out to our backyard to a green belt of land and play along Cripple Creek, where we caught crawfish with long weeds and built tree forts all along our claimed territory.

I believe that this was truly the point in time that I started on with my personal quest for fulfilment to this present day, I realised that it is the small everyday fulfilments that we all dream of that keep us going with our daily struggles.

We had moved every four years when I was a young child, moving from air base to air base captivated me. The adventure of traveling to different places and seeing our country in travel was one of the greatest cultural experiences of my lifetime. It still thrills me to this day to pick up, take off and go someplace at a moment's notice.

Our family's final move to California when I was 13 years old had even more adventures in store for me as I grew into my teenage years, with all the challenges that go along with finding out about yourself as a teenager.

I had learnt through the years, moving from air base to air base, to pick out good friends. I learnt that kids who were respectful and outgoing to others were the kids I wanted to be friends with.

I had brought my nationwide educational experience with me as a military brat, remembering and seeing first hand at home how the sacrifices of loved ones effected military family's during the time of war.

Consoling friends who lost a father in Vietnam, was the most difficult time during my military cultural experience. I'm sure it must of been the same at most post, air bases and ports throughout the world... It came down to helping one another through experiences in death, learning and seeing how others respected one another in time of tragedy.

Being proud to be in a military family, I remember the unspoken bond and strengths of our military family.

As a kid, I remember playing in a middle of a ballgame at the air base little league park. We would all stop in unison, mid game, as the evening taps started to play on the base loud speakers. We would all face the direction… knowing we're the main flag pole was on base, even if we could not see the flag from we're we were.

We would take our caps off, put them over our hearts in respect for those who had fallen that day, as the war raged on in Vietnam. To me, that is why I have so much respect for our flag and why I get angry when others disrespect the flag.

Our American flag is the symbol of freedom and when lowered, I always remember the ultimate sacrifice that all military serviceman or women, brother or sister, husband or wife or friend… who gave all for our freedoms today through the centuries… as I was able to simply continue to play ball in a park that evening. That is what I think of when I see our American flag.

I also remembered the first time I witnessed racism as a young child in Mississippi. The disrespect to the people of colour was unknown to me when I moved there.

Being raised by good parents who taught me right from wrong, we knew the culture in Mississippi was wrong and we talked about it, staying clear of family's and kids who were 'wrong-minded', as my parents put it to me as a child.

I personally stayed clear of children who were 'wrong-minded', who were taught to hate to do the peer pressures of wrong-minded families and the ignorance of others who spread hate.

Never forgetting that hot summer day at the gas station… the day my brave father took a stand against a car load of racists, as I witnessed my brave father stand up for what was right…

Living free is not always as free as we may all think… Sometimes the price of freedom is to fight for the injustices seen before us.

The peace of our freedom may need to be interrupted at times, and only we the people can take a stand against tyranny when it is set in place before us… to hopefully vote out the unreasonable or arbitrary abuse of power before it's too late.

Chapter 19
Quest for Fulfillment

My parents were always there for myself and my siblings throughout our whole lifetimes—without question. And without question, we were all there for our father as his health started to take a turn for the worse during the Christmas holiday of 2010 and throughout the New Year of 2011.

I was available to help my parents and felt like it was a blessing at that time. My parents' tri-care insurance with the military service had hospice care and there was a hospital bed provided that we had set up in the dining room of my parents' home.

There was a wonderful nurse assigned to my father, who would come by and monitor my father's health, keeping us informed of the different stages of decline.

There were good days reflecting on the memories past with my father, going over stories, laughing as we said our long goodbyes.

My father knew when his health took a turn for the worse and he told me that it would not be long; he knew when it was time.

He explained to me that his last wish would be to make it to Valentine's Day and take the whole family out to dinner to celebrate our lives together… to see the whole family together one last time.

I had done all I could do in helping out around our family home to make it easier for my parents, as I made my way to my new job as a finish carpenter, working evenings out of town.

We were all set up for what was to come, with the nurse informing us that Dad might die in the following weeks and that she would know when it was time to get us all together as we went on with our own lives.

Knowing my father's wish to make it to Valentine's Day, I had prayed for this to happen. If there was anything in my life that I would want for him, it was for him to make it to Valentine's Day dinner with his family.

The weeks went by as I worked out of town, until Valentine's Day was upon us. All the family got together as planned at my parents' home and we all loaded up in our cars to make the trip to the restaurant.

The dinner at the restaurant was the best. We all sat at a large table that was put together, with all of us kids and grandkids sitting around laughing and carrying on in conversation. We were all having a great meal with my parents at the head of the table. My father's wish had come true.

The weeks that followed were a blur to me. Working out of town was the last place that I wanted to be when I had heard the news that Dad's health had taken another bad turn at the end of February of 2011.

I received a call from Mom telling me that the nurse had explained to her to get the family together, that the time had come. I drove home that day after work.

I spent the afternoon and one point of the evening going to my father's bedside to hold his hand to say goodbye for the night. He was in and out of consciousness as I told him that I loved him. All of a sudden, he rearranged our hand grasp and shook my hand.

He did not say a word. It was all he could do at the time to shake my hand, as if to say goodbye one last time.

I went back to work that same evening on a night shift, thinking of my father at work. While I was to drive back home the next morning to be by Dad's bedside.

I received a phone call; it was from my brother Jimmy, explaining that our father had passed away in his sleep early in the morning.

I told my brother that I loved him, that I would be home soon, and that I was driving home.

We hung up and I started to cry, pulling off of the freeway onto a side road in Dixon, California. I drove the back roads thinking of him, with the brightest sunrise that I had ever witnessed in my life.

I knew that my father was at peace, and there was a peace that had fallen over me the like of which I had never felt before, as if my father himself was present in my life at that moment, looking over me.

I got home to my three brothers and my mother at our father's side, as the deacon of our church showed up to perform the last rites.

It was the first time that I could remember us all being together as a family since our teenage days, with just my brothers and me together as a family one last time, as if we had gone back in time to the days of our youth.

I felt like I was 12 years old again at our family home, looking for my father's advice one last time as he lay in peace in total silence.

The deacon seemed to go into a trance, in deep prayer over my father's body, as we said the Lord's Prayer over him together—one last time as a family.

All the arrangements were made in advance. My father was cremated, with some of his ashes given to each of us boys to do with as we wished.

The rest of his remains were interned at the Sacramento Valley National Cemetery in Dixon, California, where I unknowingly pulled off of the freeway on the way home, the morning that I heard of my father's death.

He showed us how to live our lives to the fullest and to dream as we each grew into manhood.

My family was shown the example set by my father one last time, with how he died with dignity, a life very well lived until the end.

Once you lose a loved one, you will realise—in life as in death—that life is one of the greatest fortunes your parents could have ever given you, and a grounded life of a good family upbringing were the steppingstones to self-improvement to carry you through your never-ending quest for fulfilment.

The End